Cakes at their best
© Piffz, 2016
www.piffz.com

1. edition, 1. printing
Printed in EU 2016

ISBN 978-87-93084-27-8

© 2016 Author: Patricia Olivia Stewer

Cover and graphic design:
Yummp Design Studio - www.yummp.net

 PIFFZ

Cakes at their best

by Patricia Olivia Stewer

www.piffz.com

Index

Intro

I have created this cookbook since I love to bake and be in my kitchen. I am not particularly into fine raw materials or ecology, but enjoy creating nice and tasty foods in my kitchen for my family and our friends.

This book was created only with sweets, as it's always nice to have something sweet ready when guests are coming. I have kept my focus on the easy sweets and something tasty.

All my recipes are tested by children and adults.

I wish you a good experience.

Orange Cupcakes

Approx. 12 Cupcakes

260 g flour

250 g sugar

1/2 tsp salt

2 tsp baking powder

2 large eggs (yolks and whites separated, and whites whipped stiff)

1 tsp vanilla sugar

100 g orange juice

125 g butter (softened)

PREPARATION

Preheat oven to 175 °C.

Mix butter, sugar, egg yolks and vanilla in a bowl until the mixture is creamy. Mix flour, salt and baking powder in another bowl and add gradually while stirring together with orange juice.

Whip egg whites until stiff and fold into batter.
Fill the batter into muffin molds until these is approx. ½ full.

Bake in the middle of the oven for approx. 15-20 minutes.
Let cool on a wire rack and decorate the cold orange cupcakes with orange frosting. (See next page)

Orange Frosting

For ~12 cupcakes

200 g powderes sugar
1 pinch salt
1 tbsp orange peel (grated)
70 g soft butter
2 tbsp orange juice

PREPARATION

Mix all the ingredients together and stir thoroughly.

If the frosting is too thick, it can be adjusted with an additional tablespoon of orange juice.

Cola Frosting

For ~12 cupcakes

INGREDIENTS

20 g cocoa powder

130 g cola

100 g butter

400 g powdered sugar

handful of pecans
(finely chopped)

1 tsp vanilla sugar

PREPARATION

In a medium saucepan mix cocoa, cola and butter together over medium heat until butter is flourted.

Remove pan from heat and add icing sugar, pecans and vanilla sugar. Mix well.

Keep in cold storage until it is stiff enough to get on top of your cupcakes.

Cupcakes with Cola

Approx. 12 Cupcakes

INGREDIENTS

250 g cola

125 g butter

100 g vegetable oil

20 g cocoa powder

20 large marshmallows

350 g flour

500 g sugar

1 tsp baking powder

1 tsp vanilla sugar

200 g butter milk

2 large eggs

PREPARATION

Preheat oven to 175 degrees and prepare your cupcakes molds.
Take a small saucepan and mix cola, butter, oil and cocoa. Bring mixture to a boil and remove from heat.

Add the marshmallows and put a lid on the pot until the marshmallows begins to melt. Mix.

Mix flour, sugar and baking powder in a large bowl. Add the buttermilk, eggs and vanilla and mix well.

Add the cola mixture and toss it all to you have a nice, plain dough.
Fill the batter into cupcakes molds until they are ½ full.

Put the cakes in the oven and bake for about 20 minutes.
Cool cake completely before you decorate them with cola frosting.

Button Cookies

Approx. 45 Cookies

INGREDIENTS

370 g soft butter

150 g sugar

1 egg

2 tsp vanilla sugar

3 tsp baking powder

500 g flour

ADDITIONAL

1-2 bags of chocolate
lenses (M&M's or Smarties)

PREPARATION

The ingredients are mixed together, roll dough into balls the size of a hazelnut, put on plate and a chocolate lens pressed firmly in each cookie before baking.

Bake at 175 to 200 ° C for 10-15 minutes.

Home is the ♡

Twisted Cookies

Approx. 30 Cookies

Start by taking grains out of the vanilla and crush it around in a little sugar so that the grains divide. Save it for later.

Mix the flour, sugar and butter together into a dough. Divide the dough into two equal parts. Mix one portion with 2 tbsp. cocoa and the other with the vanilla sugar you just made.

INGREDIENTS

The bright and dark dough is rolled out, laid on top of each other and rolled together as a roulade. Cut cake into 5 mm thick slices and arrange them on a plate lined with baking paper.

300 g flour

70 g sugar

300 g butter

2 tbsp cocoa

Grains from 1 vanilla pod

Bake in center of oven at 175 ° C for approx. 7-9 minutes. You must keep an eye on them so they do not get too dark.

Oat Cookies

Approx. 20 Cookies

INGREDIENTS

50 g butter

200 g oatmeal

140 g sugar

1 egg

1 tbsp flour

1/2 tsp vanilla

1 tsp baking powder

PREPARATION

Melt butter and pour it hot over the oatmeal. Add sugar, eggs, flour, vanilla and baking powder.

Put the dough into small peaks on a baking sheet. They get big and flat in baking.

Bake at 175° C for approx. 10-12 minutes

Chocolate "Yummy"

For 8-10 people

INGREDIENTS

2 eggs

270 g sugar

4 tbsp cocoa

1/2 tsp salt

Grains from 1 vanilla pod

Grated peel from 1/2 orange

85 g flour

1/2 tsp baking powder

100 g melted butter

PREPARATION

Beat eggs and sugar white. Mix cocoa, salt, vanilla, orange peel, flour and baking powder and fold into egg mixture.

Mix in the cooled butter in the end.

Pour the mixture into a greased pan and bake at 190°C for 20-25 minutes. The cake will seem unbaked. Serve for dessert with icecream.

Coco Muffins with Chocolate

Approx. 12 Muffins

INGREDIENTS

375 g flour

3 1/2 tsp baking powder

50 g desiccated coconut

165 g sugar

90 g melted butter

125 g yoghurt natural

50 g milk

2 eggs

95 g chocolate drops

GARNISH

Chocolate chips

PREPARATION

Turn oven to 190 °C .

Mix flour, coconut, baking powder, sugar
and chocolate pieces in a bowl.
Beat butter, eggs, yoghurt and milk
in a bowl and add the flour mixture.

Pour the batter into the molds with
two spoons and garnish with
chocolate pieces.

Bake in center of oven for 20 minutes.

Delicious butter
for your Muffins

For ~12 muffins

*If you feel like you are missing a little
extra for your muffins, you can easily
make some delicious butter that taste great.*

Here are 3 examples.

Bailey's Butter

For ~12 muffins

INGREDIENTS

150 g butter

175 g powdered sugar

3 tsp Bailey's

PREPARATION

Whip butter and Bailey, together with a hand mixer to have a smooth consistency. Add the powdered sugar gradually.

If necessary, use a pastry bag to decorate your cupcakes with the delicious butter

Orange
Butter

For ~12 muffins

INGREDIENTS

150 g butter

175 g powdered sugar

3 tsp finely grated
orange peel

3 tsp orange juice

PREPARATION

Whip butter, orange peel and orange juice with a hand mixer to have a smooth consistency. Add the powdered sugar gradually.

If necessary, use a pastry bag to decorate your cupcakes with the delicious butter

Vanilla Butter

For ~12 muffins

INGREDIENTS

150 g butter

175 g powdered sugar

1 tsp good vanilla sugar
or grains from a vanilla pod

PREPARATION

Whip Vanilla and butter with a hand mixer to have a smooth consistency. Add the powdered sugar gradually.

If necessary, use a pastry bag to decorate your cupcakes with the delicious butter